W9-AFG-345

American Lives

Theodore Roosevelt

Rick Burke

Heinemann Library
Chicago, Illinois

© 2003 Heinemann Library
a division of Reed Elsevier Inc.
Chicago, Illinois

Customer Service 888-454-2279

Visit our website at www.heinemannlibrary.com

Created by the publishing team
at Heinemann Library

Designed by Ginkgo Creative, Inc.
Photo Research by Kathryn Creech
Printed and Bound in the United States by
Lake Book Manufacturing, Inc.

07 06 05 04 03
10 9 8 7 6 5 4 3 2 1

Acknowledgments
The author and publishers are grateful to the
following for permission to reproduce copyright
material: pp. 4, 6, 7, 8, 9, 11, 27, 28 Theodore
Roosevelt Collection, Harvard College Library; p. 5
AP/Wide World Photos; pp. 10, 12, 18, 24 Corbis;
p. 13 Farrell Grehan/Corbis; pp. 14, 17, 22, 26
Bettmann/Corbis; p. 15 Pach Brothers/Corbis; p. 19
North Wind Picture Archives; p. 20 Oscar White/
Corbis; p. 23 Underwood & Underwood/Corbis; p.
25 Craig Aurness/Corbis; p. 29 Jeremy Woodhouse/
PhotoDisc

Cover photograph: Bettmann/Corbis

Special thanks to Patrick Halladay for his help in
the preparation of this book. Rick Burke thanks
Susie . . . now we're each responsible for a Teddy.

Every effort has been made to contact copyright
holders of any material reproduced in this book.
Any omissions will be rectified in subsequent
printings if notice is given to the publisher.

Library of Congress Cataloging-in-Publication Data
Burke, Rick, 1957-
  Theodore Roosevelt / Rick Burke.
    v. cm. — (American lives)
Includes bibliographical references and index.
Contents: A president's funeral — Childhood — Growing up — Marriage and
sadness — Dakota — Marriage, jobs, and children — Rough Riders —
Governor — President — Four more years as president — Children and
a gift — Africa and Another Election — Remembering Roosevelt.
  ISBN 1-40340-159-4 (lib. bdg.) — ISBN 1-40340-415-1 (pbk.)
  1. Roosevelt, Theodore, 1858-1919—Juvenile literature. 2.
Presidents—United States—Biography—Juvenile literature. [1.
Roosevelt, Theodore, 1858-1919. 2. Presidents.] I. Title.
  E757 .B95 2002
  973.91'1'092—dc21

                    2002004145

Some words are shown in bold, **like this.** You can
find out what they mean by looking in the glossary.

The cover of this book shows Theodore Roosevelt
giving a speech in Evanston, Illinois, in 1903.

Contents

A President's Funeral

A six-year-old boy looks out of a second-story window in 1865. He is watching Abraham Lincoln's **funeral procession.** Lincoln, the sixteenth president of the United States, was shot a few days earlier in Washington, D.C. The boy watches hundreds of sad, crying people walk behind Lincoln's **coffin** as it is moved down a street in New York City.

Lincoln was president and the leader of the United States during the Civil War. This war was fought when some southern states wanted to start their own country. The boy read articles about the war every day.

Theodore watched the procession from his grandfather's house in New York.

This picture of Roosevelt was taken in the White House in 1908.

That boy standing at the window would grow up to be president one day. He would become a strong president, just like Lincoln had been.

His name was Theodore Roosevelt. He became a president who was well-liked by the people of the United States. But other leaders in the world also knew he was willing to fight if the United States was in danger. Theodore thought that the president should use all of his powers to protect the United States.

Childhood

Theodore Roosevelt was born on October 27, 1858, in New York City. As a child, his family called him "Teedie," but when he grew up, everyone called him "Teddy." Later, when he became president, newspaper writers called him "TR."

Teddy's father, who was also named Theodore, was a rich man. The Roosevelt family had been in New York City since 1648. Teddy had one brother named Elliott and two sisters named Anna and Corinne.

Teddy's parents, Theodore and Martha, are shown above.

The Life of Theodore Roosevelt

1858	1876–1880	1881	1898
Born on October 27 in New York City.	Attended Harvard College.	Elected to New York Assembly.	Elected **governor** of New York.

Teddy made this drawing of a rat when he was a little boy.

Teddy was a weak and shy boy who didn't leave his house much because he had **asthma.** Just walking from room to room made it hard for Teddy to breathe. Because of his asthma, Teddy didn't go to school. He learned at home instead.

Teddy loved science. He kept a **museum** in his bedroom of dead animals that had been **stuffed.** He called it the Roosevelt Museum of Natural History.

1900	1901	1904	1919
Elected vice president of the U.S.	*Became 26th president of the U.S.*	*Reelected as president.*	*Died on January 6 in Long Island, New York.*

Growing Up

Teddy's father had a gym built in one of the rooms of the family's house. Teddy used it every day and got stronger.

As Teddy got older, his **asthma** did not bother him as much. He loved to go hiking to look at and hunt animals. Reading and hunting became easier when his parents found out that he needed glasses. Teddy's glasses helped him see better.

Teddy is eleven years old in this picture of him on a family trip to Paris, France.

Boxing

Growing up, Teddy loved to box. When he was president, he would box with anyone who wanted to box, even John L. Sullivan, the heavyweight champion of the world. Teddy started wrestling instead after he hurt his eye in a boxing match.

In 1876, when he was seventeen years old, Teddy went to Harvard College. His father wanted him to study business, but Teddy wanted to learn about animals. He told his father that he would never be rich, but he would be happy.

Teddy worked hard at Harvard. He went to class and studied thirteen hours a day, but he still found time to box and wrestle, go to

dance classes, teach Sunday school, and write for the school journal. He was full of energy!

Teddy's picture was taken at Harvard in 1876. The college is located in Cambridge, Massachusetts.

Marriage and Sadness

In college, Teddy met Alice Hathaway Lee at a party. She was tall, blond, and beautiful. Teddy fell in love with her. Alice didn't fall in love with him as quickly. Teddy asked her to marry him in June 1879. She finally said she would, and they were married on October 27, 1880. Teddy was 22 and Alice was 19.

After the wedding, Teddy went to law school at Columbia University in New York City. He also wrote a book about the War of 1812, a war fought between Great Britain and the United States.

Teddy's wife Alice, shown above, said she would marry Teddy on Valentine's Day in 1880.

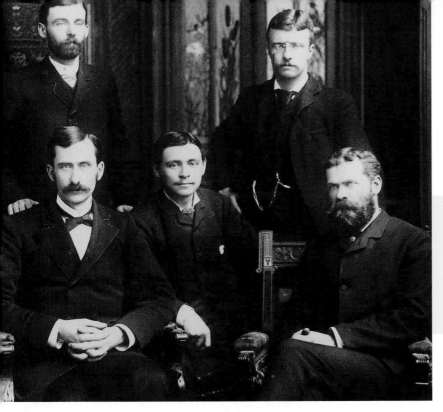

Teddy is shown here with a writer and three Assembly members. He is wearing glasses.

Teddy quit law school after a year and made money by writing more books. In 1881, three years after his father died, Teddy decided to try to get elected to the New York Assembly. This group of leaders made laws for the state of New York. Teddy won the election.

While Teddy was away working for the Assembly, Alice gave birth to a baby girl. Teddy rushed home, but when he got home he found out that both his wife and his mother were dying. They died hours apart on February 14, 1884. Alice died because her **kidneys** wouldn't work, and Teddy's mother died of **typhoid fever.**

Dakota

Teddy was very sad. He named his daughter Alice after his wife. He left the baby with his sisters and went to the **Dakota Territory** in the western part of the United States. He went there to try to get over the sadness he felt about the deaths of his mother and wife.

He bought two **cattle** ranches, the Chimney Butte Ranch and the Elkhorn. Teddy loved to be outdoors and live in nature.

Teddy went to the Dakota Territory in 1885. He is shown here wearing buckskins, a kind of clothing made from the skins of deer.

Teddy did a lot of hunting. On one trip to the Bighorn Mountains, a **grizzly bear** ran straight at him. Teddy took aim and shot the bear just before it reached him.

For a while, Teddy was a sheriff in the territory and helped **capture** outlaws.

Teddy lived in this cabin when he was at the Chimney Butte Ranch.

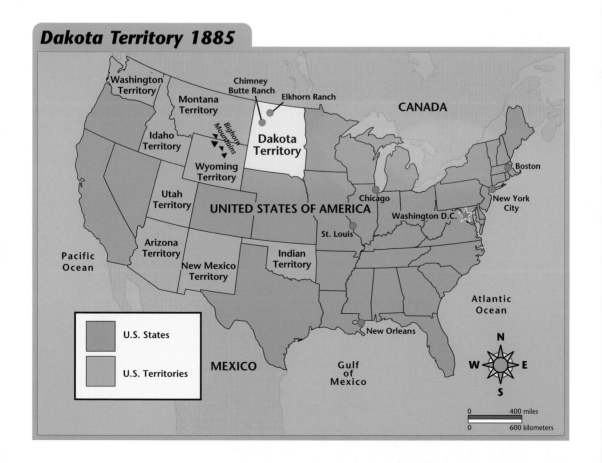

Dakota Territory 1885

Washington Territory
Chimney Butte Ranch
Elkhorn Ranch
Montana Territory
CANADA
Idaho Territory
Bighorn Mountains
Dakota Territory
Boston
Wyoming Territory
Utah Territory
UNITED STATES OF AMERICA
Chicago
Washington D.C.
New York City
Arizona Territory
St. Louis
New Mexico Territory
Indian Territory
Pacific Ocean
Atlantic Ocean
New Orleans
U.S. States
U.S. Territories
MEXICO
Gulf of Mexico

N
W E
S

0   400 miles
0   600 kilometers

Marriage, Jobs, and Children

While he lived in the West, Teddy often took train trips back to New York to see his daughter Alice. On one trip back home, Teddy fell in love again. While visiting his sister Corinne, he saw a childhood friend, Edith Kermit Carow. Teddy and Edith were married on December 2, 1886.

Teddy had been trying to get elected mayor of New York City. He lost the election, but U.S. President Benjamin Harrison wanted Teddy in Washington, D.C. Teddy's job was to get good workers jobs in the government.

Edith Kermit Carow, seen above, was a childhood friend of Teddy's. He sent letters to her from the **Dakota Territory.**

In 1895, Teddy became a police commissioner in New York City. Some police officers were not doing their jobs properly. Teddy's job was to make sure those people didn't keep their jobs. He gave good workers their jobs.

After being in New York for two years, Teddy went back to Washington, D.C. President William McKinley picked him to be assistant secretary of the U.S. Navy in 1897. By then, Teddy and Edith had six children.

Teddy and his wife Edith are seen in this picture with their children. From left to right, they are Quentin, Ted, Archie, Alice, Kermit, and Ethel.

Rough Riders

In 1898, the island of Cuba was ruled by the country of Spain. The people of Cuba wanted to be free from Spain. When a United States Navy ship, the *Maine,* exploded in the harbor of Havana, Cuba, the U.S. blamed Spain. Two months later, the U.S. went to war with Spain so Cuba could be free. Teddy quit his job and formed a group of men to fight in Cuba. The group was part of the U.S. Army and was called the Rough Riders.

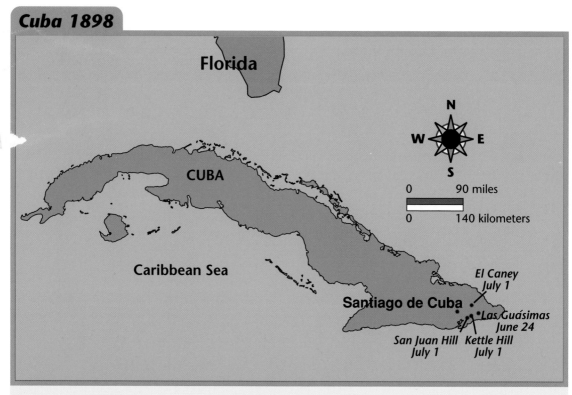

Cuba 1898

Florida

N
W — E
S

CUBA

0 ___ 90 miles
0 ___ 140 kilometers

Caribbean Sea

El Caney
July 1

Santiago de Cuba •
•Las Guásimas
June 24

San Juan Hill Kettle Hill
July 1   July 1

This map shows when and where some of the battles of the war happened in Cuba.

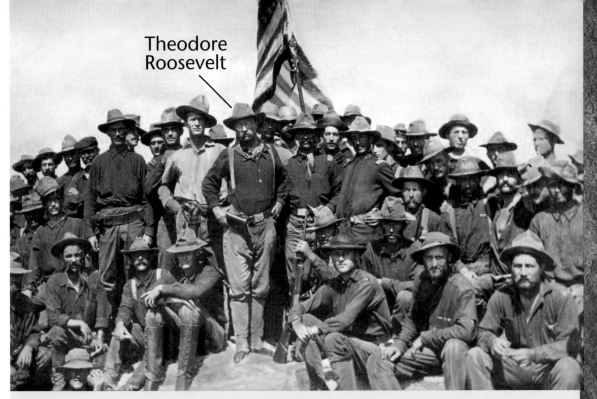

Theodore Roosevelt

In this picture, Teddy is standing with the rest of the Rough Riders after the battle. He is under the flag in the middle of the group.

On July 1, 1898, the Rough Riders **captured** a Spanish fort near Santiago, Cuba. From the fort, Teddy saw another Spanish fort near a hill called San Juan Hill. Teddy yelled for his men to run up another hill and take over the fort. The Spanish shot at them, but the Americans didn't stop. Teddy led his men and killed a Spanish soldier with his sword along the way. Teddy was hurt during the attack, but the Rough Riders took over the fort.

Governor

The United States won a great victory that day, but 100 Rough Riders died during the battle. The war ended a few weeks later. People all over the United States read about the charge up the hill that Theodore Roosevelt had led. He became a hero to the people of the country. He said later that the day of the charge was the greatest day of his life.

In this picture, Roosevelt is wearing the uniform of the Rough Riders.

Medal of Honor

In January 2001, more than 100 years after the Battle of San Juan Hill, Roosevelt was awarded the United States' highest military medal, the Congressional Medal of Honor. His great grandson Tweed accepted the medal for the Roosevelt family.

Roosevelt came back to New York and tried to get elected **governor** of the state. He won the election, but he was only governor from 1898 to 1900. An even bigger job came up.

William McKinley wanted to be elected president again. McKinley's vice president, Garrett Hobart, had died the year before. McKinley wanted Teddy to be his vice president.

Roosevelt thought the job might be boring. But he agreed because he thought being vice president might help him become president someday.

Roosevelt spoke all over the United States to get people to vote for him.

President

Roosevelt and McKinley won the election in November 1900. But then, on September 6, 1901, a man who didn't like the government shot President McKinley in Buffalo, New York. McKinley died eight days later. Roosevelt became the 26th president of the country.

Roosevelt had to come up with his own ideas of how to run the United States. He called his ideas the Square Deal and said they would make people's lives better. He wanted to stop big businesses from hurting little businesses, and he wanted to protect the **environment.**

Roosevelt is seen here with McKinley.

20

Roosevelt wanted the United States to be strong so the country could help weaker nations. Having a powerful navy was one way to be strong. The U.S. Navy became stronger when Roosevelt helped to get the **Panama Canal** built. Ships could get from one side of the U.S. to the other a lot quicker. The canal saved ships about 8,000 miles (12,875 kilometers) of sailing.

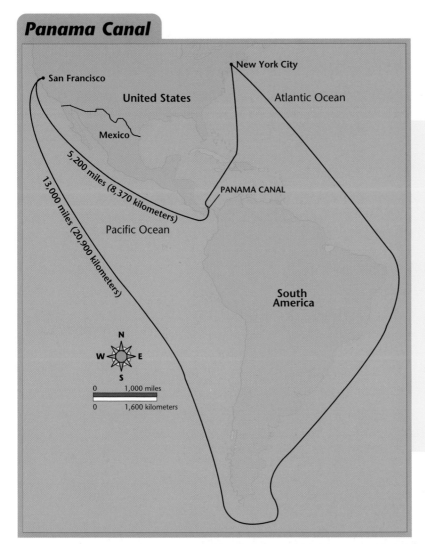

Panama Canal

- New York City
- San Francisco
- United States
- Atlantic Ocean
- Mexico
- 5,200 miles (8,370 kilometers)
- 13,000 miles (20,900 kilometers)
- PANAMA CANAL
- Pacific Ocean
- South America

N
W — E
S

0   1,000 miles
0   1,600 kilometers

Ships could sail through the canal in the country of Panama instead of sailing all the way around South America. The canal was finished in 1914 and is still used today.

Four More Years as President

In 1904, Roosevelt was elected president. During the next four years, he handled many problems with other countries.

Roosevelt thought the Monroe Doctrine was a good idea. The doctrine was named after President James Monroe. It said that the United States would not allow countries from Europe to get involved in events or problems in North and South America. To show how the U.S. could keep other nations away, Roosevelt had a group of ships, the Great White Fleet, sail around the world. The world saw how powerful the U.S. had become.

Some of the battleships of the Great White Fleet are shown here in 1907.

Roosevelt talked the Japanese and Russian leaders pictured here into stopping the war.

Roosevelt received a great honor while he was president. In 1904 and 1905, Japan and Russia fought a war against each other. They each wanted to control land in a part of China. Both countries wanted to stop fighting, but neither country wanted to be the first to stop. Roosevelt talked them into stopping the war. He was given the **Nobel Peace Prize** for helping to stop the fighting.

Roosevelt Firsts

Roosevelt was the first president to
- *fly a plane.*
- *ride in a car.*
- *visit a foreign country while president.*

Children and a Gift

People in the United States loved to read about the Roosevelt children and their adventures in the White House. They were known as the White House Gang.

Sometimes, the children rode bicycles and roller-skated in the hallways of the White House. Once, when one of the boys was sick, the other boys brought a pony into his bedroom to cheer him up.

Roosevelt took this picture of his son Quentin riding a pony in 1902.

White House

People began calling the house where the president lived the White House when Roosevelt was president. It used to be called the President's House.

Roosevelt gave a great gift to the people of the United States. He had land saved where buildings and streets could not be built. He thought the wild land of the West was beautiful and that people should be able to see that beauty for years to come.

Roosevelt helped make national forests bigger. He also created eighteen national **monuments** and five national parks. He declared the Grand Canyon a national monument in 1908.

The Grand Canyon in Arizona and the area around it became a national park in 1919.

Africa and Another Election

Roosevelt wanted to go to Europe to give speeches and get his **Nobel Prize** after he was done being president. But first, he went to Africa with his son Kermit. The Smithsonian Institute, a **museum**

Teddy Bear

On a hunting trip, Teddy refused to kill a bear that had been tied up. A shopkeeper who heard the story put two toy bears in his window and a sign that said "Teddy's bears." That's how the teddy bear got its name.

in Washington, D.C., wanted them to bring back dead animals to show in the museum.

Teddy and Kermit Roosevelt were in Africa for ten months. They shot hundreds of animals and birds for the museum to show.

Roosevelt is shown here beside an elephant he shot in Africa in 1909.

26

The thick pages of Roosevelt's speech and his eyeglass case slowed down the bullet.

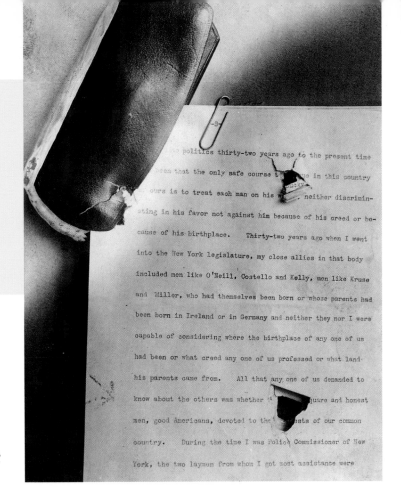

When he returned to the United States, Roosevelt was upset to find out that the new president was not using his ideas anymore. So, in 1912, Roosevelt decided to try to get elected as president again.

While Roosevelt was getting ready to give a speech in Milwaukee, Wisconsin, a man shot a gun at him. The bullet hit his eyeglass case and then hit his chest. Teddy was able to give his speech before he went to a hospital, but he lost the election to another man, Woodrow Wilson.

Remembering Roosevelt

Roosevelt wanted to fight for the United States during World War I in 1917. He wanted to lead another group like the Rough Riders. More than 200,000 men wanted to fight in the war with Roosevelt as their leader.

President Wilson did not allow Roosevelt to form an army. Roosevelt had called him a coward for not entering the war sooner. Quentin, Teddy's youngest son, was killed in the war. Quentin's

death made Teddy feel very sad, like when his first wife and mother died. On January 6, 1919, Teddy died. His heart suddenly stopped working.

The people shown here are carrying Theodore Roosevelt's **coffin.** He was buried in Long Island, New York.

Theodore Roosevelt was one of the greatest presidents of the United States. He was a man with a lot of energy, and he used that energy to make his country better and stronger.

Roosevelt cared about what happened to the poorer people of the United States. He wanted them to be able to make enough money to feed their children and live in good houses. He was a man who never stopped trying to be the best he could be.

Theodore Roosevelt

Roosevelt's face is between Jefferson and Lincoln on Mount Rushmore, along with Washington.

Mount Rushmore

Roosevelt's face is one of four presidents carved into a mountain at Mount Rushmore National Memorial in South Dakota. Each face is about as tall as a five-story building.

Glossary

asthma illness that makes it hard for a person to breathe

capture to take and hold

cattle more than one cow or bull

coffin box a person is put in after he or she dies

Dakota Territory area of land in the West that later became the states of North Dakota and South Dakota

environment all the things that surround us, including animals, weather, and plants

funeral procession group of persons who walk along in a type of parade to honor and celebrate a dead person's life before he or she is buried

governor person who is elected to lead a state

grizzly bear large, wild bear found in the western United States

kidney organ that cleans and removes waste matter from blood

monument structure, building, or area built or named to help remember someone or something

museum building or room to keep and show important things, such as paintings

Nobel Peace Prize award given to a person who helps to create peace in the world

Panama Canal waterway in the country of Panama built to shorten trips for ships

stuffed when an animal's skin is taken off and put on a frame to make the animal look like it does when it is alive

typhoid fever disease that causes fevers and sores in the intestines

More Books to Read

Kozar, Richard. *Theodore Roosevelt and the Exploration of the Amazon Basin*. Broomall, Pa.: Chelsea House Publishers, 2000.

Roosevelt, Theodore. *The Boyhood Diary of Theodore Roosevelt, 1869-1870: Early Travels of the 26th U.S. President*. Mankato, Minn.: Capstone Press, 2000.

Welsbacher, Anne. *Theodore Roosevelt*. Edina, Minn.: ABDO Publishing Company, 1998.

Places to Visit

Sagamore Hill (Roosevelt's home from 1886–1919)
20 Sagamore Hill Road
Oyster Bay, New York 11771-1807
Visitor Information: (516) 922-4447

Theodore Roosevelt Birthplace
28 East 20th Street
New York, New York 10003
Visitor Information: (212) 260-1616

Index